# THE BLACK COUNTRY
## COLOURING BOOK

First published 2017

The History Press
The Mill, Brimscombe Port
Stroud, Gloucestershire, GL5 2QG
www.thehistorypress.co.uk

British Library Cataloguing in Publication Data.
A catalogue record for this book is available from the British Library.

ISBN 978 0 7509 8243 6

Cover colouring by Lucy Hester.
Typesetting and origination by The History Press
Printed and bound in Turkey by Imak.

# THE BLACK COUNTRY
## COLOURING BOOK

PAST AND PRESENT

Take some time out of your busy life to relax and unwind with this feel-good colouring book designed for everyone who loves the Black Country.

Absorb yourself in the simple action of colouring in the scenes and settings from around the region, past and present. From historic streets and picturesque canals to scenes of the area's industrial past, you are sure to find some of your favourite locations waiting to be transformed with a splash of colour.

There are no rules – choose any page and any choice of colouring pens or pencils you like to create your own unique, colourful and creative illustrations.

Red House Cone, Dudley ▶

Wolverhampton Art Gallery ▶

Moseley Old Hall knot garden ▸

Walsall Leather Museum  ▸

Molineux Stadium ▸

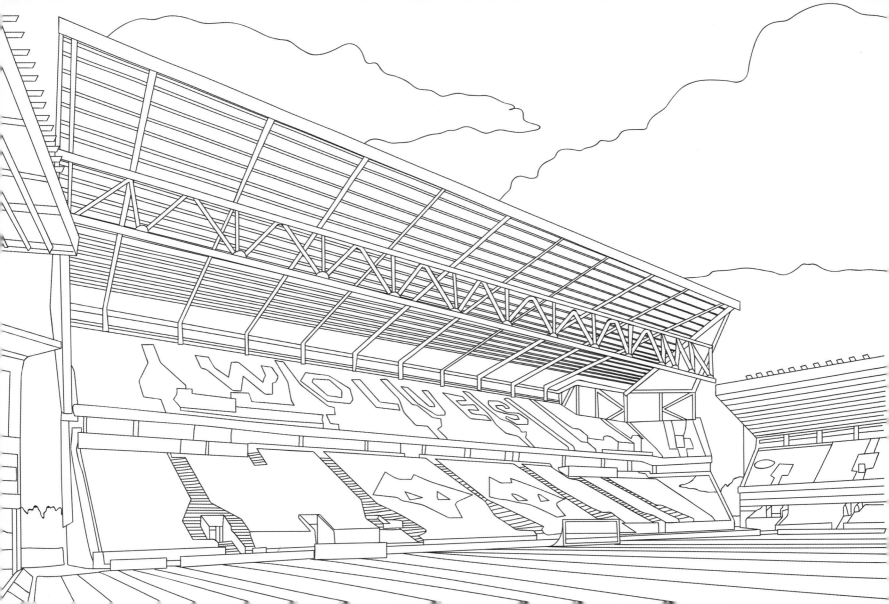

Bantock House Museum and Park ▶

Black Country Living Museum ▸

Bilston Craft Gallery ▶

Wolverhampton Corporation
trolleybus, mid-1960s  ▶

Dudley Castle ▶

Wednesbury Museum and Art Gallery ▸

Narrowboats and Walsall Art Gallery  ▶

Entrance to the castle grounds, Dudley, *c.* 1920 ▶

Delph Locks, Dudley Canal No.1 ▸

St Peter's Collegiate Church, Wolverhampton ▸

The Wildlife Trust for Birmingham & the Black Country
works to conserve biodiversity, improve the environment
and raise awareness and understanding of wildlife issues ▸

A zookeeper from Dudley Zoo walks a
camel on the slopes of Castle Hill, 1959 ▶

Haden Hill House ▶

An early view of the Fountain in
Dudley's Market Place ▶

St Mark's Church, Pensnett, known as the
Cathedral of the Black Country ▶

A GWR saddle tank engine on the
Darby End to Dudley line, 1901 ▸

Wightwick Manor, Wolverhampton ▸

Wood's Palace, Bilston, early 1920s ▶

Bloxwich War Memorial ▶

West Bromwich Albion FC's
stadium, The Hawthorns ▶

A group of colliers at one of the
Dibdale Collieries, late 1800s ▸

Black Country Living Museum ▸

Priory Park, Dudley ▸

Wolverhampton Racecourse ▶

Himley Hall ▶

Leasowes Park, Dudley ▸

Halesowen Abbey ▶

Cobb's Engine House, *c.* 1970 ▸

Dudley High Street, *c.*1920 ▶

Tipton Junction ▸

Christ Church, Oldbury ▸

Soho Foundry, Smethwick ▶

The Hawthorns, *c.* 1955  ▶

The southern end of Dudley Tunnel ▶

Market Place, Willenhall, *c.*1960 ▸

Black Country Living Museum ▶

The Oak House, West Bromwich ▶

The Black Country flag ▶

Windmill End and Cobb's engine house ▸

Also from The History Press

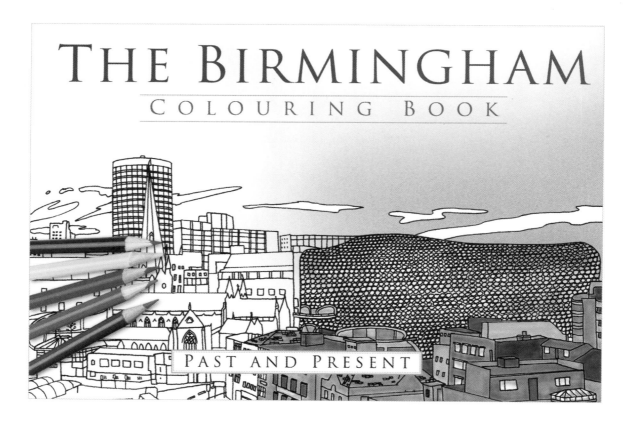